RABBITS
and Hares

A N I M A L   F A M I L I E S

RABBITS
and Hares

Annette Barkhausen and Franz Geiser

Gareth Stevens Publishing
MILWAUKEE

A N I M A L   F A M I L I E S

For a free color catalog describing Gareth Stevens' list of high-quality books, call 1-800-341-3569 (USA) or 1-800-461-9120 (Canada).

The series editor would like to extend special thanks to Jan W. Rafert, Curator of Primates and Small Mammals, Milwaukee County Zoo, Milwaukee, Wisconsin, for his kind and professional help with the information in this book.

At this time, Gareth Stevens, Inc., does not use 100 percent recycled paper, although the paper used in our books does contain about 30 percent recycled fiber. This decision was made after a careful study of current recycling procedures revealed their dubious environmental benefits. We will continue to explore recycling options.

Library of Congress Cataloging-in-Publication Data

Barkhausen, Annette.
   [Hasen, Kaninchen, und Pikas. English]
   Rabbits and hares / Annette Barkhausen and Franz Geiser; [translated from the German by Jamie Daniel]. — North American ed.
     p. cm. — (Animal families)
   Includes index.
   Summary: Introduces the physical characteristics, habits, and natural environment of various species of hares and rabbits.
   ISBN 0-8368-1004-X
   1. Lagomorpha—Juvenile literature. [1. Rabbits. 2. Hares.] I. Geiser, Franz. II. Title. III. Series: Animal families (Milwaukee, Wis.)
QL737.L3B3713 1993
599.32'2—dc20   93-15932

North American edition first published in 1994 by
Gareth Stevens Publishing
1555 North RiverCenter Drive, Suite 201
Milwaukee, Wisconsin 53212, USA

Series editor: Patricia Lantier-Sampon
Editor: Amy Bauman
Translated from the German by Jamie Daniel
Editorial assistant: Diane Laska
Editorial consultant: Jan W. Rafert

Printed in Mexico

1 2 3 4 5 6 7 8 9 99 98 97 96 95 94

Below, left: Wild rabbits spend a lot of time in burrows that they dig themselves.

Below, right: Domestic rabbits are every bit as sociable with one another as their wild relatives, and they also enjoy digging.

Table of Contents

What Is a Rabbit?

With their long ears, long legs, and short tails, hares and rabbits are unique animals – popular with people everywhere. This is proven by the many stories and customs that involve hares and rabbits. From the tradition of the Easter Bunny to the race between the tortoise and the hare plus expressions such as "quick as a bunny," numerous members of the hare and rabbit family have hopped into our everyday lives. In this book, we'll look at this family as well as that of the closely related pika, the two families that together form the order known as Lagomorpha.

Excellent Senses and Quick Legs

A legend told by the Hausa people of western Africa explains why the rabbit is always on the run. According to that legend, the moon sent the speedy rabbit to Earth to deliver a message to humankind. The rabbit was supposed to tell people that human beings must die just as the moon does so that they might be able to one day rise and live again. But the forgetful rabbit remembered only to report that people must die. As a punishment, the moon split the rabbit's upper lip. In great pain, the rabbit sprang into the moon's face and scratched it. This, in turn, explained the scars and pockmarks that you can see when you look up at the moon at night. The poor rabbit, however, was so astonished at his own actions that he ran away and continues to run through the world to this very day.

Of course, people today don't believe the rabbit is running away from the moon. Rather, we know that the rabbit is always on the run because there are so many other animals

Above and opposite, bottom: Eyes, ears, and nose — this European brown hare stands alert with all its senses scanning the surroundings.

around that like to eat rabbits. Rabbits, hares, and pikas are the favorite prey of many animals. Yet, even young rabbits or hares aren't an easy catch. In addition to their long, fast legs, they also have excellent senses that warn them early of danger. And when they can't run, lagomorphs hide or camouflage themselves.

Lagomorphs have "wide-angle" eyes. That is, the eyes are placed on either side of the head. Together, the eyes give the animal an incredibly wide field of vision. The animal is able to see what is going on in front of it, behind it, and to both its right and left — all at the same time. But one shortcoming of this wide field of vision is that the animal cannot focus very sharply on individual objects. In high grass, rabbits and hares raise themselves up on their hind legs to get a complete look at their surroundings. In the forest, they are also aided by their large ears, which help them hear extremely well. Their ears and their excellent sense of smell make it possible for lagomorphs to recognize an enemy quickly.

Although a lagomorph's ears pick up most any sound, they have another function. The ears also regulate body temperature. For example, North American jackrabbits that live in hot deserts or semi-arid regions have the largest ears. These animals use their giant ears as cooling surfaces. When it is very hot, they spread their ears wide in the breeze to cool their entire bodies. On the other hand, the pikas that live in cooler climates have the smallest ears; these serve to help the pikas stay warm.

All of the lagomorphs' sense organs are equipped primarily for detecting enemies. But their sense of smell also helps them communicate. The animals have scent glands in their mouths along the insides of their cheeks. The animals distribute the contents of these glands over their entire bodies when

Top: As is the case with many nocturnal animals, the eyes of Cape hares "light up" at night. Above: Cottontail rabbits live throughout North America.

they clean themselves. This way, each animal establishes its own smell that other rabbits or hares can recognize. Scent markings also come in the form of urine and droppings. These mark boundaries between territories in the world of rabbits, hares, and pikas.

A Special Digestive System
Rabbits, hares, and pikas don't have too much trouble finding food. All hares and rabbits are herbivores, which means they feed only on plants. And although grasses and herbs are the lagomorphs' main food source, they will also eat buds, fruit, seeds, roots, leaves, and even tree bark.

While finding food isn't a problem for lagomorphs, digesting it can be. Many of the plant foods that rabbits, hares, and pikas eat are difficult to digest. Fortunately, these animals have a special digestive system in which some foods are digested twice. As food matter passes through the small intestine, partially digested nutritious matter, known as chyme, is taken into the animal's large appendix. There, the food is further processed by bacteria. To pass these nutrients along through the animal's system, however, the food must be returned to the small intestine. To do this, lagomorphs excrete this matter in small, soft balls that are eaten again. The process of reingesting is a matter of life and death for these animals.

Family Relations

Until several decades ago, rabbits, hares, and pikas were classified as members of the

rodent family. This group includes animals such as rats, mice, guinea pigs, squirrels, gophers, beavers, and porcupines. But detailed studies have shown more differences than similarities between the rabbit group and the rodent group. Because of such differences, rabbits, hares, and pikas are now classified as members of a separate order. This order, Lagomorpha, includes two families: Ochotonidae, which is that of the pikas, and Leporidae, which includes true hares and rabbits.

The history of the lagomorphs began about fifty million years ago. At that time, the first known rabbitlike animals lived in Asia. Their hind legs were not as long as those of present-day hares and rabbits, and thus they looked more like pikas. The first true pikas, however, first appeared only about thirty million years ago. These short-eared, tailless animals look a little like guinea pigs but are not related to them. They are genuine members of the Ochotonidae family. The family Leporidae, which includes both rabbits and hares, is just as old as that of the pikas.

Hare vs. Rabbit

As members of the same family, hares and rabbits have much in common. Certain differences, however, set these two animals apart. The true hare, for example, is a free-range animal able to survive in any weather. *Free-range* means the hare doesn't burrow or build any sort of housing. Nest-building is a habit found only among types of hares that live in extraordinarily harsh climates. North American jackrabbits, for instance, stay in cool burrows in the ground during the hottest part of the day, while arctic hares and snowshoe hares build burrows in the snow.

To survive this free-range existence, young hares must be able to fend for themselves.

Below, left: A replica (4th Century B.C.) of a hare-shaped belt buckle. Below, right: A decorative sitting rabbit from the Roman Empire.

Right: A Greek hunter's return from a rabbit hunt is portrayed on the inside of an antique drinking vessel.

Unlike rabbits, hares are already well-developed at birth. Each newborn hare has a complete coat of fur, and its eyes are open. It can also move around on its own from the very beginning. This is especially important to the baby hare's survival, since the mother hare simply leaves the babies behind, usually in a natural nest heap, and returns only when it is time to nurse them.

In contrast to most hares, rabbits do burrow and nest. While some rabbits make their homes under logs, bushes, or rocks, others use holes abandoned by other animals. Still others, such as the European wild rabbit, build underground dens with whole systems of tunnels and chambers. Many of these burrows, known as warrens, are complete with escape hatches that the rabbits use if danger threatens. Steppe pikas are like rabbits in this respect. But the pikas in mountainous regions make their homes in natural hollows under tree trunks and rocks.

Whatever type of nest they use, rabbits spend a great part of their lives in their protective homes. In their homes, rabbits are able to bring their young into the world. Newborn rabbits are almost completely hairless and blind. The mother rabbit builds her young a soft nest made of straw and the soft down from her belly. In this nest, she nurses them for about three weeks.

Left: It's grooming time for this little rabbit.

10

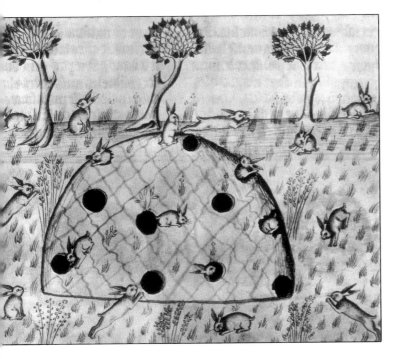

Left: *The rabbit and its life are represented in a medieval book from 1405.*

Bottom: *The well-known German painter Albrecht Dürer created this realistic image of a young hare in 1502.*

between seven and nine offspring every year. Female rabbits are even more fertile; they bear between eight and twelve offspring annually. The pikas are even farther ahead of their larger cousins when it comes to reproduction. They have twenty to thirty babies over the course of a year!

Loners and Big Families

Several members of the true hare family seem inclined to live alone. But this tendency has exceptions, as in the case of the European brown hares. These hares prefer to spend the

Survival Strategy

One characteristic hares and rabbits share is that both animals escape from their enemies by paying attention and being able to make a fast escape. The ways in which they do this, however, are very different. When a hare is disturbed, it relies first on its camouflage, then bolts like a streak of lightning at the last moment and runs away. Fortunately, the hare is not just a fast runner; it is also able to run long distances. In contrast, when danger threatens rabbits, they don't run for long distances to escape. Rather, rabbits always run in the direction that will get them back to their den the fastest.

In addition to their sharp senses and the ability to react quickly to danger, hares and rabbits share yet another characteristic that helps them survive – their ability to reproduce. Almost two-thirds of all wild hares and rabbits die within their first year of life. These losses must be offset by a large number of births if the population is to remain stable. Thus, a female field hare will bear an average of

Right, top: Widder rabbits are not as easygoing as their floppy ears might suggest. These rabbits can be temperamental.

Right, bottom: The Angora rabbit needs extensive care to keep its long hair from becoming matted.

Below: Pygmy rabbits are popular as pets.

day on their own but gather together with the group at night to eat. And arctic hares in the far north are often found living in large groups.

In contrast, wild rabbits form family groups of closely related animals in which a fixed hierarchy is maintained. These groups establish territories for themselves and will defend the territories from intruders. The animals in such a group recognize each other by their individual body odors.

The language of sounds, on the other hand, seems of only minor importance to

Darius. When a hare suddenly leaped onto the field just as the battle was about to begin, the Scythians wanted to hunt the creature. So, completely dropping their battle plans, they chased after the long-eared prey.

Breeding rabbits for meat also is a centuries-old practice. As far back as the ancient Romans, people ate rabbits for food. Domestic rabbits were first raised in French monasteries starting in about 1000 B.C. By

either rabbits or hares. When there is danger, several species sound a shrill cry of alarm. Others warn one another by loudly thumping their hind feet against the ground. Occasionally, lagomorphs make purring noises in self-defense. But, otherwise, there is little communication of the kind that can be heard among families of rabbits and hares. Pikas, however, are called "whistling hares." These lagomorphs use shrill calls day and night to communicate messages of all sorts.

A Conflicting Relationship

The relationship between lagomorphs and humans is a conflicting one. On one hand, humans help the spread of hares and rabbits by clearing forests, introducing the animals to new territories, and encouraging domestication and breeding of certain species. On the other hand, humans also limit these animal populations through hunting and altering or damaging the lagomorphs' habitat.

Hunting rabbits and hares was a popular sport even in ancient times. In the year 512, a Scythian lord attacked the Persian king

means of selective breeding, the monks were able to produce rabbits that were not afraid of humans. In the same way, they also tried to alter the animals' body size and fur color. As early as the sixteenth century, there are accounts of black, gold, and spotted rabbits.

Above: Through the docile rabbit, children can learn the responsibilities and rewards of caring for a living thing.

Today, there are over fifty different kinds of rabbits. Certain pygmy rabbits grow to an adult weight of little more than 2 pounds (1 kg), while large varieties like the German giant rabbit can weigh as much as 15 pounds (7 kg). Domestic rabbits differ from wild rabbits in body size and reproductive habits. Domestic rabbits reproduce even more often than the wild species. At the same time, the senses of domestic rabbits have been dulled considerably, and their brains are 20 percent smaller than those of their wild cousins.

Yet all of these breeds of domestic rabbit, as different from one another as they all may be, stem from the same European wild rabbit. And like their wild cousins, domestic rabbits like to live in family groups, hop around in the grass, and dig their own burrows. Domestic rabbits can be kept humanely only if they are able to take part in these "rabbit" activities.

Right: An artist's depiction of a suffering rabbit. Many brown hares suffer today in densely populated areas because of the destruction of their habitats.

Differences between Hares and Rabbits		
	Hares	**Rabbits**
ears	long, with black tips	shorter, no black tips
habitat	open fields, edges of the forest	underground burrows
babies	born fully furred with eyes open; ready to flee the nest	born hairless and blind; need to be protected in the nest
escape	long-distance run across fields	short-distance run into the burrow
group life	live as loners or in loose groups	live in strictly organized family groups

European brown hare

arctic hare

European wild rabbits

jackrabbit

A Guide to Rabbits and Hares

snowshoe hare

cottontail rabbit

red rockhare

bushman hares

Amami rabbit

pika

European Brown Hares

Scientific name: Lepus europaeus
Length, head to rump: 20-30 inches
   (50-76 centimeters)
Weight: 6-14 pounds (2.5 to 6.5 kilograms)

European brown hares are sociable animals at night. Entire family groups of hares can often be seen grazing in a field by the light of the moon. But during the day, most hares can be found safely tucked away by themselves, with each in its own hiding place.

Sometimes this hiding place is little more than a soft hollow or depression, called a *furrow*, in the ground.

Not a Scared Rabbit, Just Born to Run

A brown hare that has tucked itself away in a hiding place is hard to find. Its coat, sprinkled as it is with brown, gray, black, and white, works well as camouflage. If a clever fox, a hunting human, or any other predator comes too close, the hare will duck down low to escape the threat. At the same time, the little animal's heartbeat slows down so even the motion of breathing won't give it away. If, despite all these precautions, the hare is still discovered, its alarm system will immediately turn on. At this point, its heart will accelerate to three times its normal beat, pumping oxygen-rich blood to its muscles.

Only at the last possible moment will the hare shift into an escape mode. Taking advantage of the tension built up in its body, the animal then catapults itself into the air like a rocket. And because the hare knows its territory inside out and knows where all the escape routes are, it will often escape. Few predators — including the fox, the dog, and the wildcat — have what it takes to catch a hare that is moving at speeds of 37-43 miles (60-70 kilometers) an hour. But the hare is not only faster than many of its predators, it is also more flexible. For example, when a pursuer seems to have finally caught up with the hare, the hare will suddenly zigzag off in a different direction. Before the confused pursuer can stop and change directions, the hare has already covered a lot of ground. Only a whole pack of dogs working together is

Left: This brown hare is on the alert! Opposite, top: A perfect hare landscape — lots of different plant growth in a small space. Opposite, bottom left: A brown hare shows its black-tipped ears. Opposite, bottom right: Before running, a brown hare first tries to use its camouflage coat.

able to keep up with the hare's many twists and turns. When there is a pack, the dogs take turns following the trail. This way, when the hare makes a quick turn, most of the dogs are able to make it, too. Large groups of dogs can mean death for the hare.

Safest Without Their Mothers

Older brown hares have only a few natural enemies that pose any serious danger to their safety. Young hares, on the other hand, are the favorite prey of foxes, predatory birds,

Young brown hares are born after a gestation period of about forty-two days. As is typical of hares, the young are born with fur, and they can see and run within a short time of their birth. The mother hare will leave the young during the day as soon as they are born. After that, she will visit them only at night to give them a chance to nurse on her extremely rich milk. Because of their mother's milk, the young hares will grow quickly. At birth, they weigh about 5 ounces (140 grams). After a month, they will weigh nearly 2 pounds

Above: Male hares meet to take part in courting activities.

cats, and other such enemies. Hare populations aren't really seriously threatened by these meat-eaters, since the hares can reproduce so quickly. A female hare, called a *doe*, can give birth to as many as three or four litters per year, with as many as seven babies in each litter. The average number of babies in a litter, however, is actually two or three, with a total of between six and nine babies per year.

(1 kg). By six months, the hares will be nearly full grown.

Leaving the young alone is actually a way of protecting them. Because of her size, the mother hare could easily draw the attention of a fox or other predator. Thus, when they are left alone, the babies are well protected by their camouflage coats, their lack of identifying scent, and their smaller size. If people find a little hare on its own, they should not assume

18

that the animal is lost or abandoned and take it home with them. The little hare and its littermates most probably have not been abandoned. Their mother is simply watching from a distance.

Vanishing Habitat

For centuries, the European brown hare has enjoyed living in the forest, especially in clearings made by farmers. Hares prefer

Above, left: Brown hares sometimes fight during the mating season.

Above, right: Brown hares mate after a period of intense competition.

Above, center right: The female visits the nest to nurse her young.

Right: Young hares come into the world with a full coat of fur and open eyes.

living in open fields with occasional hedges to living in thick forests. An area's hare population usually increases as more forest land is cleared. In the past, the hare's favorite habitat was the traditional farm, where small, varied fields made up about two-thirds of the farmland. The remaining third was made up of hedges, forest border, and other uncultivated land. But meadows and fields have changed over the last decade. Farmers have planted ever-larger crops of corn and grain, keeping out certain varieties of plants that serve as food for the hare population. And farmers have sprayed the fields with deadly poisons that affect both plant and animal life.

Farmers consider dandelions, red hemp nettles, and goosefoot to be weeds. But these plants are essential sources of food and medicine to many animals. In earlier times, when the plowed fields were smaller and their

borders weren't yet being sprayed, hares fed on hundreds of weeds and grasses. But today, many areas contain only endless fields of corn that border on giant fields of wheat, neither of which meets the hares' needs.

To benefit hares, property owners should leave a little space around hedges and along the edges of fields and roads where plants can grow wild. Farmers should not plow the fields under too soon after harvesting. Farmers might also plant some clover into the fields once the corn is knee high. Any of these ideas would also benefit the farmers because it would improve the soil and lessen the risk of erosion after rainfalls.

Roads constructed by humans have cut into the hares' habitats and hindered their free movement. The hares have grown afraid of crossing wide highways and have become prisoners between them, walled into smaller and smaller areas. These animals will not

Left: In central Europe today, more hares fall victim to traffic than to the hunter's gun.

Above: Fifteen hares are the catch after a day's hunt.

Opposite, top: Father and son hunt hares together. Such hunting doesn't inflict much serious damage on the hare population.

survive under these circumstances. They need to be able to gather at night for their group feedings.

Fortunately, hares don't really like to take long trips. A family of hares actually needs only about .4 sq. mile (1 sq. km) of land to exist. As long as the land has a sufficient supply of weeds and grasses for the animals to eat and plenty of underbrush for hiding, these hares will survive.

During the mating season from spring until fall, however, male hares will travel long distances to find females. At this time of year, hares won't hesitate to cross busy streets. Many hares lose their lives because of this.

Above: Because of their long, powerful hind legs, brown hares can reach a speed of about 43 miles (70 km) per hour.

Left: No two brown hares are exactly alike. Coloring can vary greatly.

Arctic Hares

Scientific name: Lepus timidus
Length, head to rump: 19-27 inches
   (48-69 cm)
Weight: 6-7 pounds (2.5 to 3 kg)

Above: When the arctic hare grows its winter coat, only the tips of its ears and the tips of its toes have dark fur.

About two million years ago, the Earth cooled down a great deal. The Ice Age began, and glaciers extended from the polar regions to the mountains and even onto the plains.

Giant forests were destroyed. In areas the glaciers didn't reach, only sparse grass and bushes grew. A group of hares adapted to life in this cold, harsh environment; these animals were the ancestors of today's arctic hares.

Arctic hares, also called snow hares, can be distinguished from brown hares by their smaller size, their rounder bodies, their shorter ears, and their snow-white tails. They also grow a white winter coat. Only the tips of their ears and their toes stay dark. In the spring, most arctic hares change coats again, turning back into brown hares. Some arctic hares that live very far to the north, however, stay white all year round.

An International Society
When the Ice Age ended about ten thousand years ago, arctic hares followed the retreating glaciers and split up into several different population groups. Their most heavily populated habitat is the tundra grasslands that run from Siberia across Scandinavia up into Greenland and the North American Arctic. Some researchers consider arctic hares in Canada and Alaska a species all their own. But there is much evidence to support the claim that these animals are only a large subspecies of arctic hare.

A group of Ice Age arctic hares followed the retreating glaciers as far as central Europe. There they became the ancestors of the Alpine snow hare. Other Arctic hares survived in the Scottish highlands and in Ireland.

All arctic hares basically prefer the same sort of surroundings with sparse plant growth and a long, cold winter. The farther south they live, the higher they have to climb to find these living conditions. Thus, arctic hares live in the tundra of the far north, while their Scottish relatives can be found at heights of 984-3,937 feet (300-1,200 m) above sea level. Alpine snow hares must climb as high as 9,843 feet (3,000 m) above sea level.

live in winter on tree bark, pine needles, and thin branches. They also eat all sorts of twigs, as well as seeds and pine cones.

Arctic hares can build up mountains of snow and make tunnels in them for shelter. Alpine snow hares, on the other hand, prefer to hide in natural hollows under rocks and boulders. Arctic hares in Canada and

At Home in Snow and Ice

Arctic hares are well equipped for long, snowy winters. Then, their white winter coats make them nearly invisible to their enemies. To avoid sinking into the snow, their wide hind paws grow a layer of stiff, straight fur on their soles. This way, the hare's paws act like snowshoes to help the animal travel across the snow. Although arctic hares love to eat grasses and weeds in the summer, they can

Above, left: Arctic hares hide in natural hollows under rocks and branches.

Above, right: This year, the snow came early and caught the arctic hare still wearing its summer coat.

Right: Wide back paws make it possible for the arctic hare to walk across the snow without sinking.

Greenland gather in the winter in groups of dozens or even hundreds of animals. If danger threatens, the whole group hops away. Some hares leap distances as long as 6.5 feet (2 m) through the snow.

Not Endangered Despite the Difficulties

In their harsh environment, arctic hares face many difficulties. Like all animals, they suffer from people's tendencies to use their habitats for winter sports. The hares also have to watch for eagles, hawks, owls, ravens, and foxes. In the far north, they must be wary of wolves, arctic foxes, and snowy owls.

Despite such dangers, arctic hares are not endangered animals. Although they are not found anywhere in great numbers, their territorial range makes it likely that they will survive. Because the animals are so good at hiding themselves, biologists will probably never have an accurate population estimate.

Above: Young arctic hares are left alone by their mothers until feeding time.

Above, right: The arctic hare always has white feet, even in summer.

Right: In spring, the arctic hare's coat begins to change.

Jackrabbits

Scientific name: Lepus (various species)
Length, head to rump: 17-26 inches
   (43-66 cm)
Weight: 6-13 pounds (2.5-6 kg)

Several species of North American hares with especially long ears are called jackrabbits. One of these is the antelope jackrabbit, whose ears take up almost a fourth of its entire body surface. The ears are very important in regulating the animal's body temperature. Jackrabbits usually live in areas in which there are extreme variations in temperature. When it is cold, the animal will keep its ears flat against its body to prevent as much heat loss as possible. On the other hand, if the animal is overheated, it will raise its big ears to get rid of the excess heat through the ear surfaces. When it is very hot at midday, antelope jackrabbits rest in the cool shadows of their burrows.

An unusual type of behavior has been observed in antelope jackrabbits. When fleeing a predator, this jackrabbit, like most jackrabbits, moves in a bounding, zigzag pattern. As an antelope jackrabbit runs from an enemy, however, it exposes a patch of white fur on its rump. This sudden flash of white fur against the brown over the rest of the hare's body is thought to confuse the pursuer and serve as a communication of danger to other jackrabbits as well.

The black-tailed, or California, jackrabbit is the fastest species of jackrabbit. As fast as this animal can run, however, its speed does not seem to intimidate the many coyotes, foxes, and otters that hunt it. To help balance the hare's population despite losses to such predators, a female black-tailed jackrabbit usually has four to five litters a year with two babies in each. This jackrabbit lives on the

Above: Of all the lagomorphs, the jackrabbit has the longest ears. Here, a black-tailed jackrabbit washes its face.

plains and in the deserts of the western United States and in Mexico. It is also found in areas where cattle are raised. The black-tailed jackrabbit is especially fond of cultivated plants and has earned a reputation as a pest with farmers because of the heavy damage it does to crops. In winter, this jackrabbit survives mainly on a diet of branches. If necessary, it will also eat cactus, nibbling at the plants until nothing is left but the spines and the tough undersides of the plant.

Snowshoe Hares

Scientific name: Lepus americanus
Length, head to rump: 14-20 inches
   (36-52 cm)
Weight: 2-4 pounds (1-2 kg)

them rose and fell in regular cycles of eight to eleven years. At the height of the cycle, several thousand snowshoe hares populate every .4 sq. mile (1 sq. km) of land. The population then quickly drops until only a few hundred animals populate that same area. At this point, the animals begin reproducing again.

The snowshoe hare, popularly called the snowshoe rabbit, lives in the forests of Alaska, Canada, and the northern United States. This animal's name comes from its wide hind feet, which, like snowshoes, help the hare walk across its snowy habitat. The snowshoe hare is famous among biologists because of its population, which rises and falls in a regular pattern. Even a century ago, Canadian fur traders noticed that the number of snowshoe hare furs that trappers delivered to

The fur traders also discovered that the number of lynx, one of the hare's major predators, rose and fell in the same pattern. This is because the predator population drops with a shortage of its food supply — the snowshoe hare. Sick and weakened by a lack of food, the lynx population then decreases within about a year of a similar shift for the snowshoe hare.

Above: Unlike the arctic hare, the North American snowshoe hare lives in forests.

European Wild Rabbits

Scientific name: Oryctolagus cuniculus
Length, head to rump: 15-20 inches
   (38-50 cm)
Weight: 2-4 pounds (1-2 kg)

Another World

If we could see into the ground, we would see an entire world built under the ground. Beneath the ground at the end of a long passage might be a small burrow lined with grass, moss, and the soft down from a rabbit's underbelly. In this little nest might be three blind, deaf, and hairless baby rabbits. They might have come into the world yesterday. The pink-skinned bunnies get restless and wriggle in the warm nest material, positioning themselves for nourishment. This is important, for as soon as the mother rabbit arrives, the baby rabbits will begin to nurse eagerly. Although they are usually only able to nurse for a total of about two minutes a night, the babies will triple their birth weight of 1.4-1.5 ounces (40-45 g) in about three weeks. At this point, they will have fur, be able to see, and be ready to leave the nest for the first time. After a month, they will be pushed out of the nest to make room for their mother's next litter.

After cleaning herself up, the mother rabbit, or doe, goes out again in search of food. Once outside the den, she may be spotted by a male rabbit, or buck. Does are able to mate and conceive again as soon as they have given birth, so the buck takes off after her. She zigs and zags around the meadow with the buck staying just behind her at a short distance. Once she is sitting still, the buck will hop up beside her with a strange, stiff-legged hop and try to win her heart by showing her the white underside of his stubby tail. The pair will stay close together, sometimes rubbing their noses together and grooming each other's heads. If the doe is then ready to mate, she will.

After a gestation period of one month, the little rabbits are born. Usually, there will be five or six in a litter. Yet more than half of all rabbit pregnancies don't result in births.

Above: It is almost impossible to tell the difference between male and female rabbits just by looking at them. Female rabbits, however, are usually a little heavier.

Instead, the unborn young are released from the womb and reabsorbed into the mother's body. Biologists don't know for certain why some pregnancies end this way. It might be nature's way of controlling the rabbit population. Nonetheless, every doe will bear between eight and twelve young every year.

27

Strict Rules for Big Families

A rabbit is rarely seen on its own. Rabbits prefer to live in pairs or in colonies. Generally, a colony consists of six to twelve animals. Within the colony, males and females maintain a strict hierarchy. The leader is the strongest male, and he is paired off with the highest-ranking female. But as the predominant male, the leader will also mate with other females in the colony. Thus, the lead male is responsible for the majority of the offspring. The highest-ranked female is the only female allowed to raise her young in the common family burrow. Her offspring will have a much better chance at survival than those of the other mothers. These offspring will be raised in makeshift nests off from the main area of the burrow.

Top: The ground around a rabbit colony looks like a piece of Swiss cheese. Above: Many animals can live in a small space. Opposite: Whether standing (top) or returning to the burrow (bottom), the rabbit is always alert.

borders of the territory with scent markings from the glands in his cheeks. Droppings also contain this scent. In addition, all members of the colony family are sprayed with urine by this male. This establishes a group odor. If a strange buck happens to enter the marked-off territory, he will be attacked fiercely by the lead male.

The Colony's Neighborhood

One sign of a nearby rabbit colony is an area of short grass. The grass surrounding the colony is often clipped short as a result of the rabbits' special grazing technique. Sitting just outside the burrow, a rabbit will carefully eat the grass using a right-to-left, back-and-forth motion. It moves slowly forward until it can't reach any farther by extending its head. Then it hops one step forward and starts the process again. A group of five to seven rabbits can eat as much grass as one sheep.

But rabbits are actually more fond of weeds than grass. They will also eat cultivated grains and fruit, peel bark from trees, and

A colony's territory will rarely cover more than 50 acres (20 hectares). In densely populated areas, as many as twenty-seven to thirty-seven rabbits may live on a single acre of land. Within the territory, the colony's living area is built up around a central, shared structure. It is usually built underground and consists of several passageways and rooms with several entrances and exits. One important entrance goes in a straight, up-and-down direction. It is used by the rabbits when they have to make quick getaways from enemies. Rabbits that live in wet underbrush or sandy areas are not able to build such burrows. They have to live out in the open like hares.

The highest-ranking male is responsible for defending the territory. He marks the

raid vegetable gardens. Because of their wide, almost indiscriminate diet, rabbits can easily destroy the plant life on small islands. Rabbits introduced to the Kerguelen Islands in the Indian Ocean, for example, have eaten almost all of the Kerguelen cabbage — a plant native to the area.

Little Invaders Conquer the World

Rabbits can be found as far south as the South Pole, but they originally were found only in southern Europe and in a small area of northwestern Africa. Romans colonizing the area that is now Spain learned to value the animal as a source of meat. To be sure that there would always be enough rabbit meat, the Romans began to keep rabbits in cages. They also released rabbits on various islands in the Mediterranean. Even before the birth of Christ, the inhabitants of the Balearic Islands were asking for help from Emperor Caesar Augustus because the rabbits had devoured all their harvests!

Rabbits, like hares, can thank people for their present-day territorial range. During the Middle Ages, people enjoyed the taste of rabbit meat and also kept them in cages. These rabbits extended across all of central and western Europe as far as England. Rabbits that escaped and readapted to life in the wild reproduced rapidly. Rabbits continued to be introduced by people into new areas, whether on islands to provide a food source for passing ships and sailors or as animals to hunt in newly colonized lands.

In some instances, the introduction of rabbits to an area has had catastrophic results. Australia's experience is an example of this. There, the rabbits seemed quite harmless at first. In fact, two attempts to introduce them in the late eighteenth century failed. Then in 1859, a ship brought twenty-four rabbits to Melbourne. These animals, and some that followed soon after them, survived. Four years later, with few predators

to control the population, rabbits began to overly populate the continent. By the turn of the century, they were everywhere. Only areas without a good water supply were spared from the invasion. Rabbits were also reproducing during the same period in New Zealand and Chile. In the Andes Mountains

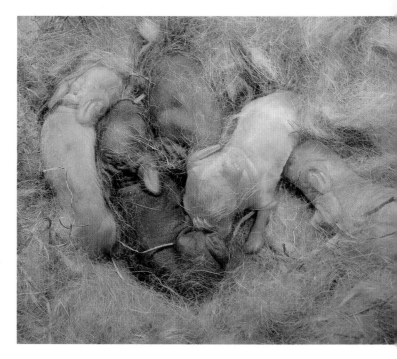

Only a few days and a couple of meals stand between these hairless newborns (top) and the cute balls of fur they become (bottom).

of South America, rabbits learned to live in areas as high as 6,562 feet (2,000 m) above sea level.

By 1950, Australia's natural landscape and its agriculture were suffering under the burden of an estimated 600 million rabbits. Native animals that were also herbivores were starving to death because the rabbits were eating all the food. Farmers could not feed their herds of sheep and cattle. The worst damage, however, was done to the plants. Because plant growth rates couldn't match the pace at which the plants were being eaten, gaps in the plant cover began to appear. As a result, valuable soil was carried away by wind and rainwater.

The Australian people made desperate attempts to control the rabbit population.

Above: **In twenty-one to twenty-five days, young rabbits venture out of the burrow for the first time.**

Below: **It is rare to see a mother and her young together like this.**

They were spending huge sums of money to fight the plague of rabbits — hunting them, fencing them out, and poisoning them. Finally, in 1950, a disease deadly to domestic rabbits was discovered in South America. This disease, myxomatosis, is caused by a virus carried by blood-sucking insects and passed by contact between animals. The Australians grasped at this disease as a means of ending their rabbit plague. After several difficulties at first, the Australians succeeded in infecting the rabbit population with the myxomatosis virus. The disease spread quickly, devastating the population.

And yet, after suffering great initial losses, the quiet creatures persist. Surviving animals have slowly developed a partial immunity to the disease. But today, the rabbit population in Australia is a reasonable size.

Above: This animal suffers from the rabbit disease myxomatosis. *Swollen eyelids and a puffy head are signs of this deadly sickness.*

Below: A massive increase in the rabbit population can have drastic effects on the plant cover, as seen in this aerial photo.

Cottontail Rabbits

Scientific name: Sylvilagus (various species)
Length, head to rump: 8-18 inches (20-45 cm)
Weight: 8 ounces-4 pounds (225 g-1.8 kg)

On several occasions, hunters tried to introduce European wild rabbits into North America for hunting. But the foreign rabbits never took hold, perhaps because America is already firmly populated by the cottontail rabbit. In North America, a dozen varieties of this rabbit inhabit all different regions of the

Below: Like most of its cousins, the Audubon cottontail rabbit prefers to sit in a slight hollow in the ground rather than dig a burrow.

United States. They thrive in all sorts of environments — deserts, fields, woods, swamps, brushlands, prairies, and even parks. In South America, two varieties of cottontails are found — the Brazilian tapeti (or forest rabbit), and the eastern cottontail rabbit in the northeastern part of the country.

The eastern cottontail is found wherever people live. This rabbit is even at home in the gardens and parks of America's big cities. The males of this species follow a strict hierarchy. High-ranking bucks can mate with the females whenever they are ready to mate. Generally, females mate four or five times a year. The hairless offspring come into the world just twenty-eight days later. Unlike most of their relatives, however, the young cottontails are not born in a burrow, but in a simple hollow in the ground. There, the nest

has been carefully lined with soft hay, leaves, and soft fur from the mother's underbelly. The mother nurses her five or more babies three times every night. For the rest of the time, the young are left alone, although they are first carefully covered up for safety. In three or four weeks, the young rabbits are

What the water is to the marsh rabbit and the swamp rabbit, the underbrush is to the brush rabbit. These little cottontails never stray any farther from their safely covered habitat than about 39-43 feet (12-13 m).

The smallest cottontail, the pygmy rabbit, lives in burrows that it digs for itself

ready to eat on their own. Cottontails are fully grown by about five months.

Swamp rabbits and marsh rabbits live in marshes, swamps, and coastal regions and are excellent swimmers. If a marsh rabbit senses danger, it will jump into the water and hide between the plants. There the rabbit will sit quietly with only the tip of its nose sticking above the water. The nests of both of these types of rabbits are always found just above the flood line.

throughout the Great Basin plains of the western United States. The pygmy rabbit is a clever creature and, like most types of cottontails, likes to stay in one area. This rabbit rarely leaves the cover of underbrush that is typical in its habitat.

Above: Although the Audubon cottontail rabbit prefers to live in the wide, unpopulated desert, it can also be found near human settlements.

Red Rockhares

Scientific name: Pronolagus (various species)
Length, head to rump: 16-20 inches
   (40-50 cm)
Weight: 3-6 pounds (1.5-3 kg)

Red rockhares are found only in southern Africa. They spend their days in their holes, which are often protected by a jagged rock. In late afternoons and evenings, they emerge to feed. These hares munch on grass, weeds, and young crops, but prefer the fresh new grass that grows on the plains. There, large

A red rockhare sits motionless under a rocky overhang. The color of the animal's fur blends completely with the background. A skillful hunter could catch the animal by hand at this point, for red rockhares will often stay in their hiding places until it is too late to run, as if rooted to the spot. Frequently, though, the hunter who thinks he has the rockhare within his grasp will find himself left with nothing but a pile of fur (rockhares lose their fur very easily).

groups of these animals come together to graze. Although red rockhares typically live in colonies, each animal has its own hideaway.

During the mating season, several bucks will follow a female. She will bear a litter of one or two hairless young about one month later in a well-concealed nest. The young are born primarily during the summer.

Above: Red rockhares cuddle in the dark.

Bushman Hares

Scientific name: Bunolagus monticularis
Length, head to rump: 14-18 in. (36-46 cm)
Weight: 2-5.5 pounds (1-2.5 kg)

"Bushman hares move slowly and awkwardly, like newborn lambs. Their tails hang down between their hind legs. They run so slowly that any dog would be able to catch them." This short description was written by G. C. Shortridge, a man who spent nearly twenty years of his life studying bushman hares. The animals were discovered in the Karoo highlands of South Africa in 1902, but then were not seen again until 1929. When Shortridge, a museum curator, began his search to find them again after 1929, he knew only that they supposedly lived on mountain cliffs. He searched for the animals until 1947, when he got lucky. By chance, he came upon a group of bushman hares on a riverbank, and he captured four of them. These would be the last bushman hares to be captured for another thirty-one years.

As they are extremely rare, bushman hares are endangered animals. They live along rivers, where they hide in the thick bushes. Nothing is known about their reproductive behavior.

Amami Rabbits

Scientific name: Pentalagus furnessi
Length, head to rump: 17-20 in. (43-51 cm)

These rabbits are found only in the dense forests of the Amami island group, the northernmost of the Japanese Ryukyu Islands. In the early twentieth century, these animals were hunted aggressively because people enjoyed their tasty meat and used the rabbits as test animals. Since then, however, they have been fully protected by the Japanese government.

Their nocturnal habits and their rarity have for the most part kept the Amamis from curious researchers. It seems the female gives birth to between one and three hairless young every year. They live in self-dug hollows that are about 3 feet (1 m) long. Analyses of stomach contents have revealed that they feed primarily on bamboo seedlings, leaves, and the vines of sweet potatoes and berries.

Above, left: Bushman hares live along riverbanks that are increasingly being used by humans for agriculture.

Above, right: Amami rabbits have unusually long claws.

Volcano Rabbits

Scientific name: Romerolagus monticularis
Length, head to rump: 11-14 in. (27-36 cm)
Weight: 14-19 ounces (400-540 g)

The volcano rabbit lives 9,843-13,123 feet (3,000-4,000 m) above sea level in the cliffs of the Mexican Popacatepetl and Ixtacihuatl mountains. It is found only in this area, in the grassy undergrowth of the evergreen forests. Its entire territorial range is no larger than 98 acres (40 ha), which is about the size of a small farm.

These small, dark animals look something like the pika, or calling rabbit. Volcano rabbits have relatively small ears and no visible tail. They are primarily nocturnal but can also be seen taking sunbaths in the cool morning or after heavy rain. Volcano rabbits may live in burrows they dig themselves, or they may live in safe spots under rocks.

Above ground, the volcano rabbits build a complex network of paths between tall tufts of zacaton grass. The young grass shoots also serve as a primary food source for these little rabbits.

Above: Volcano rabbits communicate with different whistling sounds.

The following rabbits are known to exist, but, to date, extensive research has not been done on them:

Bristly Hares

Scientific name: Caprolagus hispidus
Length: Up to 19 inches (48 cm)
Weight: 6 pounds (3 kg)

These rabbits have coarse, bristly coats. They live alone in grassy undergrowth along the borders of forests at the southern foot of the Himalayan Mountains. Because farmers often burn off this grass, the rabbits look for food on the cultivated land. For this reason, these rabbits are heavily hunted and are presently threatened with extinction.

Bunyoro Rabbits

Scientific name: Poelagus majorita
Length: 17-20 inches (44-50 cm)
Weight: 4-7 pounds (2-3 kg)

These nocturnal rabbits live in rocky, grassy areas in the central African savanna. They are territorial and will defend their turf if threatened. Commonly, one rabbit burrow is occupied by a pair of Bunyoro rabbits or by a mother and her young.

Sumatran Rabbits

Scientific name: Nesolagus netscheri
Length: 14-15 inches (36-38 cm)

The only lagomorph with a striped coat, this rabbit's fur is rusty red with black stripes. The animal is found only in the mountain forests of Sumatra. It is extremely rare and is currently threatened with extinction.

Pikas
(or Calling Rabbits)

Scientific name: Ochotona (various species)
Length, head to rump: 5-10 in. (12-25 cm)
Weight: 3.5-15 ounces (100-425 g)

look more like big-eared guinea pigs. In fact, pikas have neither long ears nor elongated hind legs. Pikas are also known for their loud calls or whistles. This is one characteristic other lagomorphs don't share. Although most lagomorphs do use some vocalization — such as an alarm call when danger strikes —

Today's pikas, also known as calling rabbits, are the last surviving members of a group of animals that were strongest twenty million years ago. There once were at least seventeen types of pika in Asia, Europe, North America, and Africa. Today, only the genus Ochotona survives, but this single genus contains about fourteen species. Most pikas live in Asia, although two species live in North America.

Most people wouldn't recognize the pikas as animals of the lagomorpha order. They

pikas use their calls for other reasons as well. The job of gathering food for winter, for example, is accompanied by "harvesting calls." And male pikas use "whistling songs" to guard their territory.

Most pika species live in elevated areas. Some make their homes on rocky slopes more than 13,124 feet (4,000 m) high. In spite of the harshness of such habitats, however, pikas do not hibernate. Instead, these little animals gather and store food to see them through the winter. Much of the pika's day is spent collecting green plant stems, drying them in the sun, and dragging the plant matter beneath a rocky overhang, where it is stored. Only two species of pika do not store food. Both of these species, the Royle's pika and the large-eared pika, live in the Himalayan Mountains. These pikas are able to find fresh food all year round, either because they live in areas in which there isn't much snow or because there is still food to be found under the snow cover.

In Russia, pikas are called "haystackers." This is especially true of the animals that live on the steppes — the steppe pika and the Daurian pika. These two species do not live in holes or under rock shelters like many other pikas do. Instead, they live in self-dug burrows. These pikas will gather and store large mounds of hay near their burrow. These mounds can weigh as much as 13-18 pounds (6-8 kg). Because these stores grow so enormous, they are often spotted and stolen by other animals, such as antelopes. Sometimes, even local shepherds make off with the pikas' hay.

Pikas live in colonies and are diurnal, which means they are active during the day. In fact, most pika varieties seem most active in the early morning hours. Then the males are known to sit on their "singing rocks" or in front of their burrows and just sing. Other males must respect these territorial announcements and stay away. Pikas are often found living in pairs or in groups. Some animals will come together like this only during the mating season. Afterward, the males and females split off into their own areas. Each group claims its own territory and builds its own haystacks. An exception to this tendency are the Mongolian pikas. These animals prefer to live in large colonies and build one giant haystack that is shared by the entire group.

Opposite: Even while eating, a pika must be on guard against enemies such as weasels, foxes, and predatory birds.

Right, top: An Altai pika stands guard.

Right, bottom: A North American pika carries supplies for the winter.

The Easter Bunny

In many parts of the world, children wake up early on Easter Day and search through backyards and gardens for Easter eggs and other small gifts. These eggs and gifts, according to custom, have been prepared and hidden by the Easter Bunny, and they represent the new life that begins in the spring season each year. In Europe, this custom began with the Easter Hare. In North America, however, people eventually renamed it the Easter Rabbit or Easter Bunny.

The custom of Easter eggs goes back to a pre-Christian fertility ritual. Because rabbits are so fertile and because eggs are such a good representation of the birth process, many primitive people believed that eating eggs delivered by rabbits would help a woman have several children. This isn't true, of course, but this is how rabbits and eggs came to be associated with magical beliefs.

When Christianity spread from Palestine through Europe, the old legends about rabbits took on a Christian interpretation. People brought eggs to church to be blessed by a priest. At this time, even the rabbit became a religious symbol for some people, as can be seen in certain art from that time. A painting in the Muottatal cloister in Switzerland shows three hares that are supposed to represent the Holy Trinity. A picture by German artist Albrecht Dürer shows a shocked hare watching as Eve takes a bite of the forbidden apple in Eden.

For centuries, the egg has symbolized new life about to begin. So on Easter Day, legend has it that the Easter Bunny brings eggs to those who believe in the birth process. These brightly painted eggs, which can also be made of chocolate or sugary candy, delight children everywhere as they celebrate the rites of spring.

This Easter bunny is made of delicious chocolate.

APPENDIX TO ANIMAL FAMILIES

RABBITS
and Hares

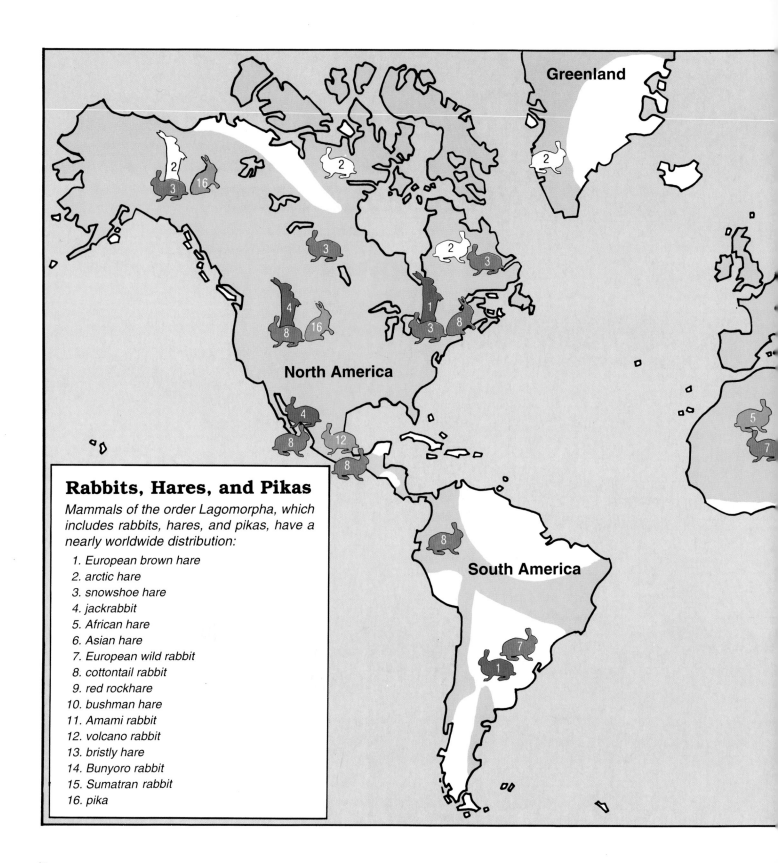

Rabbits, Hares, and Pikas

Mammals of the order Lagomorpha, which includes rabbits, hares, and pikas, have a nearly worldwide distribution:

1. European brown hare
2. arctic hare
3. snowshoe hare
4. jackrabbit
5. African hare
6. Asian hare
7. European wild rabbit
8. cottontail rabbit
9. red rockhare
10. bushman hare
11. Amami rabbit
12. volcano rabbit
13. bristly hare
14. Bunyoro rabbit
15. Sumatran rabbit
16. pika

Greenland

North America

South America

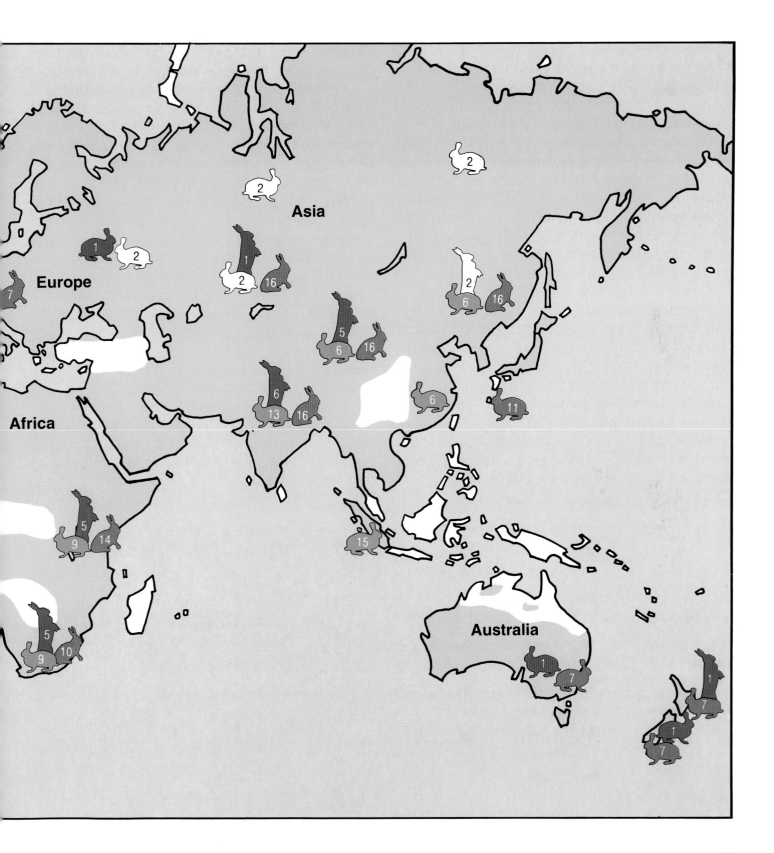

ABOUT THESE BOOKS

Although this series is called "Animal Families," these books aren't just about fathers, mothers, and young. They also discuss the scientific definition of *family,* which is a division of biological classification and includes many animals.

Biological classification is a method that scientists use to identify and organize living things. Using this system, scientists place animals and plants into larger groups that share similar characteristics. Characteristics are physical features, natural habits, ancestral backgrounds, or any other qualities that make one organism either like or different from another.

The method used today for biological classification was introduced in 1753 by a Swedish botanist-naturalist named Carolus Linnaeus. Although many scientists tried to find ways to classify the world's plants and animals, Linnaeus's system seemed to be the only useful choice. Charles Darwin, a famous British naturalist, referred to Linnaeus's system in his theory of evolution, which was published in his book *On the Origin of Species* in 1859. Linnaeus's system of classification, shown below, includes seven major categories, or groups. These are: kingdom, phylum, class, order, family, genus, and species.

An easy way to remember the divisions and their order is to memorize this sentence: "Ken Put Cake On Frank's Good Shirt." The first letter of each word in this sentence gives you the first letter of a division. (The *K* in *Ken,* for example, stands for *kingdom.*) The order of the words in this sentence suggests the order of the divisions from largest to smallest. The kingdom is the largest of these divisions; the species is the smallest. The larger the division, the more types of animals or plants it contains. For example, the animal kingdom, called Animalia, contains everything from worms to whales. Smaller divisions, such as the family, have fewer members that share more characteristics. For example, members of the bear family, Ursidae, include the polar bear, the brown bear, and many others.

In the following chart, the lion species is followed through all seven categories. As the categories expand to include more and more members, remember that only a few examples are pictured here. Each division has many more members.

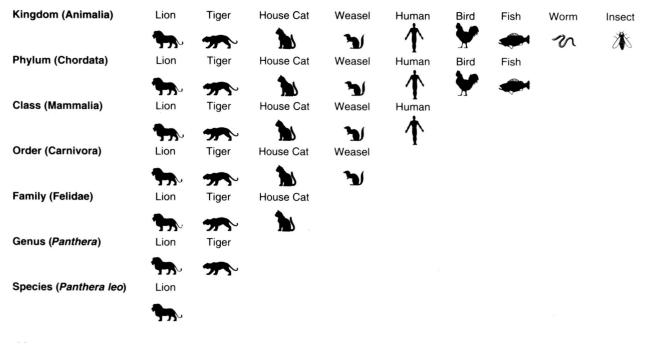

Kingdom (Animalia)	Lion	Tiger	House Cat	Weasel	Human	Bird	Fish	Worm	Insect
Phylum (Chordata)	Lion	Tiger	House Cat	Weasel	Human	Bird	Fish		
Class (Mammalia)	Lion	Tiger	House Cat	Weasel	Human				
Order (Carnivora)	Lion	Tiger	House Cat	Weasel					
Family (Felidae)	Lion	Tiger	House Cat						
Genus (*Panthera*)	Lion	Tiger							
Species (*Panthera leo*)	Lion								

SCIENTIFIC NAMES OF THE ANIMALS IN THIS BOOK

Animals have different names in every language. For this reason, researchers the world over use the same scientific names, which usually stem from ancient Greek or Latin. Most animals are classified by two names. One is the genus name; the other is the name of the species to which they belong. Additional names indicate further subgroupings. Here is a list of the animals included in *Rabbits and Hares.*

European brown hare	*Lepus europaeus*
Arctic hare	*Lepus timidus*
Jackrabbit	*Lepus (various species)*
Snowshoe hare	*Lepus americanus*
European wild rabbit	*Oryctolagus cuniculus*
Cottontail rabbit	*Sylvilagus (various species)*
Red rockhare	*Pronolagus (various species)*
Bushman hare	*Bunolagus monticularis*
Amami rabbit	*Pentalagus furnessi*
Volcano rabbit	*Romerolagus monticularis*
Bristly hare	*Caprolagus hispidus*
Bunyoro rabbit	*Poelagus majorita*
Sumatran rabbit	*Nesolagus netscheri*
Pika (or Calling rabbit)	*Ochotona (various species)*

GLOSSARY

bucks
The males of some animal species.

burrow
A hole in the ground made by an animal for shelter. Within the Lagomorpha order, the use of a burrow is one feature that separates rabbits from hares. Whereas many rabbits will either dig a burrow or use that of another animal, hares do not burrow.

camouflage
To conceal or hide by disguise. The color and markings of many animals, including many lagomorphs, hide them from enemies by helping them blend into the natural surroundings.

diurnal
Active mainly during the day.

doe(s)
The female(s) of some animal species.

domesticate
To adapt an animal or plant to live and breed in tame conditions. Rabbits have been domesticated for hundreds of years. All domestic breeds are descended from the European wild rabbit (Oryctolagus cuniculus).

double digestion
The digestion process undertaken by all lagomorphs. In the process, the animals pass food material through their digestive systems twice to properly break down the difficult plant matters in their diets.

extinction
Condition in which a specific living organism (plant or animal) is completely destroyed or killed off. Many animals that once thrived in the world are now extinct. Many others, because of factors such as the destruction of their habitats, unregulated hunting, and even the introduction of competitive species, currently face the tragedy of extinction.

family
The fifth of seven divisions in the biological classification system proposed by Swedish botanist-naturalist Carolus Linnaeus. Animals of the order Lagomorpha are grouped in two families – Ochotonidae, which is that of the pikas, and Leporidae, which include true hares and rabbits.

furrow
A small hollow or depression in which a hare rests during the day.

genus (plural: genera)
The sixth division in the biological classification system proposed by Swedish botanist-naturalist Carolus Linnaeus. A genus is the main subdivision of a family and includes one or more species.

gestation period
The number of days from actual conception to the birth of an animal. Gestation periods vary greatly for different types of animals. Within the order Lagomorpha, gestation periods of four to six weeks are common.

habitat
The natural living area or type of environment in which an animal normally lives.

herbivore
An animal whose diet consists of plants.

hierarchy
An established order within a group by which its members function. Rabbits living in large groups often function with an established hierarchy led by the strongest, most dominant buck.

incisors
The long front teeth of an animal that are adapted for cutting. While rodents have only four front teeth or incisors, rabbits and hares have an extra pair of incisors in their upper jaws.

kingdom
The first of seven divisions in the biological classification system proposed by Swedish botanist-naturalist Carolus Linnaeus. Rabbits, pikas, and hares all belong to the kingdom Animalia.

Lagomorpha
The scientific order to which hares, rabbits, and pikas belong. Members of this order can be found nearly everywhere throughout the world, with the exception of Antarctica and Madagascar, in habitats that range from desert to arctic.

Leporidae
One of two families that make up the scientific order Lagomorpha. This family includes both rabbits and true hares.

litter
The young of an animal that are born at a single point in time.

myxomatosis
A disease, spread by mosquitoes, that affects rabbits. This often deadly disease has been used to control overabundant rabbit populations.

nocturnal
Active mainly at night.

Ochotonidae
The scientific family to which pikas belong. This family is one of two families in the Lagomorpha order.

order
The fourth of seven divisions in the biological classification system proposed by Carolus Linnaeus. The order is the main subdivision of the class and contains different families. The animals discussed in this book belong to the order Lagomorpha.

Rodentia
A scientific order of small, gnawing animals such as rats, mice, and squirrels. Members of this order are known for their sharp, constantly growing front teeth, or incisors. Rabbits, hares, and pikas were once thought to belong to this order but have since been classified as members of an independent order known as Lagomorpha.

species
The last of the seven divisions in Carolus Linnaeus's biological classification system. The species is the main subdivision of the genus. At the level of species, members share many features and are capable of breeding with one another.

steppe
A large, flat, treeless area of land.

warren
A usually complex system of tunnels where rabbits live, breed, and socialize. This network may accommodate hundreds of animals.

MORE BOOKS ABOUT RABBITS, HARES, AND PIKAS

All About Rabbits. Howard Hirschhorn (T.F.H. Publications)
Discovering Rabbits and Hares. Keith Porter (Watts)
Harper & Row's Complete Field Guide to North American Wildlife. Henry Hill Collins, Jr. (Harper & Row)
(See guide appropriate to your area.)
Rabbits. Monika Wegler (Barron's)
Rabbits: All About Them. Alvin and Virginia Silverstein (Lothrop, Lee & Shepard)
Rabbits and Other Small Mammals. Charles Osborne, Editor (Time-Life Films)
World Guide to Mammals. Nicole Duplaix and Noel Simon (Crown Publishers, Inc.)
The World of Rabbits. Jennifer Coldrey (Gareth Stevens)

PLACES TO WRITE

The following are some of the many organizations that exist to educate people about animals, promote the protection of animals, and encourage the conservation of their environments. Write to these organizations for more information about rabbits, hares, pikas, other animals, or animal concerns of interest to you. When you write, include your name, address, and age, and tell them clearly what you want to know. Don't forget to enclose a stamped, self-addressed envelope for a reply.

American Rabbit Breeders
   Association
P.O. Box 426
Bloomington, IL 61702

Canadian Wildlife Federation
2740 Queensview Drive
Ottawa, Ontario K2B 1A2

The Nature Conservancy
1815 North Lynn Street
Arlington, VA 22209

THINGS TO DO

These projects are designed to help you have fun with what you've learned about rabbits and hares. You can do the activities alone, in small groups, or as a class project.

1. Spend some time observing a domestic rabbit in a pet store, at a fair, at a friend's house, or wherever you can find one. Then the next time you see a wild rabbit or hare, spend some time observing it. Take notes on everything you observe during your encounters. When did you see the rabbit/hare? What was the animal doing when you saw it? Was it alone or part of a group? What differences do you notice between the two animals? In what ways are the two animals alike?

2. At the next county or state fair, locate the domestic rabbits exhibit. Make a list of items you notice about the many breeds. Which breed is the biggest? Which is the smallest? Which type of rabbit is the most unusual? Which type do you like best? Why?

3. Visit the petting zoo of the zoo nearest you. Rabbits often are among the animals you will find there.

4. Imagine you are going to raise and breed a specific animal such as a rabbit. What information would you need to know? What major decisions would you face?

INDEX